ROSEN ✓ V

U.S. GOVERN

THE ELECTORAL COLLEGE

Carol Hand

ROSEN
PUBLISHING

New York

Published in 2021 by The Rosen Publishing Group, Inc.
29 East 21st Street, New York, NY 10010

Copyright © 2021 by The Rosen Publishing Group, Inc.

First Edition

Editor: Siyavush Saidian
Book Design: Reann Nye

Photo Credits: Cover (map Puwadol Jaturawutthichai/Shutterstock.com; cover (flag) Sergey Kamshylin/Shutterstock.com; series Art PinkPueblo/Shutterstock.com; p. 5 skynesher/iStock/Getty Images Plus/Getty Images; p. 7 Hill Street Studios/DigitalVision/Getty Images; p. 9 txking/Shutterstock.com; p. 11 Sean Locke Photography/Shutterstock.com; p. 13 Hulton Archive/Getty Images; p. 15 https://commons.wikimedia.org/wiki/File:Scene_at_the_Signing_of_the_Constitution_of_the_United_States.jpg; p. 17 MPI/Archive Photos/Getty Images; p. 19 Pacific Press/LightRocket/Getty Images; p. 21 mark reinstein/Shutterstock.com; pp. 22–23 Mike Derer/ASSOCIATED PRESS; p. 25 John Sommers II/Getty Images News/Getty Images; p. 27 ZACH GIBSON/AFP/Getty Images; p. 29 Mark Makela/Getty Images News/Getty Images; pp. 31, 41 Maps Expert/Shutterstock.com; p. 33 (Jefferson) https://commons.wikimedia.org/wiki/File:Official_Presidential_portrait_of_Thomas_Jefferson_(by_Rembrandt_Peale,_1800)(cropped).jpg; p. 33 (Adams) https://commons.wikimedia.org/wiki/File:John_Adams,_Gilbert_Stuart,_c1800_1815.jpg; p. 33 (Q. Adams) https://commons.wikimedia.org/wiki/File:JQA_Photo.tif; p. 33 (Jackson) https://commons.wikimedia.org/wiki/File:Andrew_jackson_headFXD.jpg; p. 35 UniversalImagesGroup/Universal Images Group/Getty Images; p. 37 Darren McCollester/Hulton Archive/Getty Images; p. 39 Joe Sohm/Visions of America/Universal Images Group/Getty Images; p. 43 Jeff J Mitchell/Getty Images News/Getty Images; p. 45 Hill Street Studios/DigitalVision/Getty Images.

Library of Congress Cataloging-in-Publication Data

Names: Hand, Carol, 1945– author.
Title: The Electoral College / Carol Hand.
Description: New York : Rosen Publishing, [2021] | Series: Rosen verified:
    U.S. Government | Includes index.
Identifiers: LCCN 2020000871 | ISBN 9781499468571 (paperback) | ISBN
    9781499468588 (library binding)
Subjects: LCSH: Electoral college—United States—Juvenile literature. |
    Voting—United States—Juvenile literature.
Classification: LCC JK529 .H33 2021 | DDC 324.6/3—dc23
LC record available at https://lccn.loc.gov/2020000871

Manufactured in the United States of America

Some of the images in this book illustrate individuals who are models. The depictions do not imply actual situations or events.

CPSIA Compliance Information: Batch #BSR20. For Further Information contact Rosen Publishing, New York, New York at 1-800-237-9932.

Find us on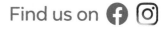

CONTENTS

TWO WAYS TO VOTE

Most elections are decided by **popular vote**. For example, if you ran for class president at school, everyone's vote would count.

Each person gets one vote. If there are two **candidates**, the winner needs a **majority**—more than half of the votes. If 100 people vote, and at least 51 of them vote for you, you win the election! If there were three or more candidates, you'd just need to win more votes than the other people. You wouldn't need a majority.

One important election isn't decided by popular vote. This is the election for president and vice president of the United States. A group called the Electoral College uses **electoral votes** to pick the president.

Classroom elections are often decided by popular vote.

DIFFERENT RULES FOR THE HIGHEST OFFICE

Elections for president are held every four years. They occur on the Tuesday after the first Monday in November. The president and vice president are elected together. They run on the same ticket.

People do not vote directly for the president. They vote for a group of **electors**. The electors then vote for the president. The vote is indirect.

Each state has a group of electors. The number of electors in each state is based on population.

✅ VERIFIED

Hosted by the House of Representatives, this site gives an overview of the Electoral College:
https://history.house.gov/Institution/ Electoral-College/Electoral-College/

Voters cast indirect votes in presidential elections. They vote for electors.

WHAT IS THE ELECTORAL COLLEGE?

The Electoral College is a group of people who directly elect the president. Political parties choose electors for each state. Each elector gets one electoral vote.

There are 538 electors in the United States. The 50 states have 535. The District of Columbia has 3.

Every state has at least three electors. Each state gets the same number of electors as it has senators and representatives. Each state has two senators and at least one representative.

FAST FACT
AT FIRST, ONLY STATES HAD ELECTORS. THE 23RD AMENDMENT TO THE CONSTITUTION ADDED THREE ELECTORS FOR THE DISTRICT OF COLUMBIA.

This chart shows an Electoral College vote count for the 2016 election.

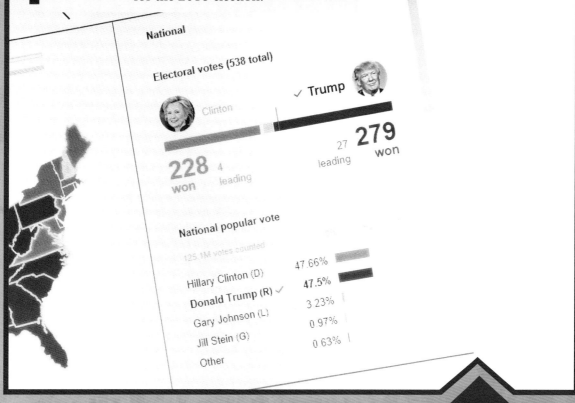

National

Electoral votes (538 total)

✓ Trump

Clinton

228 won   4 leading

27 leading   **279** won

National popular vote

125.1M votes counted

Hillary Clinton (D)	47.66%
Donald Trump (R) ✓	**47.5%**
Gary Johnson (L)	3.23%
Jill Stein (G)	0.97%
Other	0.63%

STATES WITH THE MOST ELECTORS:

- California (55)
- New York (29)
- Texas (38)
- Florida (29)

STATES WITH ONLY THREE ELECTORS:

- Alaska
- Delaware
- Vermont
- North Dakota
- South Dakota
- Montana
- Wyoming

WHAT THE CONSTITUTION SAYS

The words "electoral college" are not in the U.S. Constitution. The Constitution does describe "electors." Article II states how to choose electors. It tells how electors will vote for president and vice president. The candidate with the most electoral votes will be president. The candidate with the second-most votes will be vice president.

The 12th Amendment was passed in 1804. It changed this electoral process. It states that electors will vote separately for president and vice president.

Presidential elections have changed in other ways too. For example, state electors are now chosen by popular vote.

The U.S. Constitution describes the process of electing a president.

COMPROMISE

The Founding Fathers disagreed about how to choose the president and vice president. Some wanted Congress to choose them. A few wanted them chosen by popular vote. The Electoral College was a **compromise**. Each side got part of what they wanted.

FINDING A MIDDLE GROUND

Most Founding Fathers wanted an electoral college. George Mason of Virginia was one of them. When the Constitution was written, people lived far from each other. Travel was hard. Letters were slow. Mason thought ordinary citizens would not know the candidates well enough to elect a president.

Mason helped write the Constitution. He refused to sign it because it did not include a Bill of Rights. James Madison, who later wrote the Bill of Rights, used many of Mason's ideas.

George Mason supported people's rights.

ELECTORAL COLLEGE: WHY? WHY NOT?

Like Mason, most Founding Fathers wanted indirect presidential elections. They disagreed on how to set up the Electoral College, though.

People worried that the new government would limit their power. States with few people worried that larger states would control who became president.

Large states wanted to base the number of electors on population size. This is how the House of Representatives is set up. Smaller states wanted an equal number of votes for all states, like the Senate. The Electoral College does both.

MAKING STATES HAPPY

The design of the Electoral College addressed many issues, including the following:

- It partly limited the power of large states.

- It allowed states to vote for their own electors.

- It allowed state electors to cast their own votes for president.

- If there was no majority, the House would choose the president.

The Founding Fathers signed the Constitution in 1787.

THE ELECTORAL COLLEGE AND SLAVERY

The Constitution was written in 1787. At that time, 40 percent of people in southern states were slaves. They could not vote. Only a few southerners could vote. They were mostly male plantation owners and farmers.

Most voters lived in northern cities, such as Boston and Philadelphia. Southerners were afraid northern states would have all the power. To make things more equal, they wanted to count slaves in their population, even though slaves couldn't vote.

OLD VOTING RULES

Today, most citizens over age 18 can vote. In 1787, only white male property owners could vote. Women weren't allowed to. Most black Americans were slaves and couldn't vote either.

Many Founding Fathers, including George Washington, owned slaves.

People in the northern states said slaves were treated as property, not people, in the south. The writers of the Constitution compromised. They decided to count each slave as three-fifths of a person. They used this fraction when dividing states into congressional districts and when choosing electors.

THE RULES KEEP CHANGING

People have always objected to the Electoral College. People have tried to change it many times by changing the Constitution. Few changes have been successful.

In 1804, the 12th Amendment to the Constitution passed. It led to the president and vice president being elected on separate ballots.

Until 1961, citizens of the District of Columbia couldn't help choose the president. They had no electoral votes. The 23rd Amendment gave the District of Columbia three electors.

In 1969, a bill was introduced in Congress to eliminate the Electoral College. It said the president and the vice president should be elected directly. The bill passed the House of Representatives but failed in the Senate.

RAISING OBJECTIONS

Objections to the Electoral College increase when a candidate wins the popular vote but loses the electoral vote. So far, these objections have not led to change.

People protested the 2016 election results when the Electoral College and popular vote disagreed.

HOW DOES IT WORK?

Every four years, a presidential election is held on the Tuesday after the first Monday in November. Voters select one presidential candidate on the ballot. But they're actually choosing their state's electors.

The winning electors meet on the first Monday after the second Wednesday in December. They vote separately for president and vice president.

On January 6 of the next year, all members of Congress meet together. This is called a **joint session**. They count the electoral votes from all states. The vice president watches the vote and announces the results.

On January 20, the president-elect is sworn in as president of the United States.

Vice President Dan Quayle oversees the counting of electoral votes in the 1992 election.

PICKING ELECTORS

The Constitution outlines who can't be an elector. U.S. senators, representatives, and anyone employed by the U.S. government can't be. No one can be an elector if they've ever betrayed the country.

Political parties nominate electors. They often choose people active in the party. They sometimes pick state senators or representatives. In the general election, individuals are voting for these electors.

✔ VERIFIED

You can find more about the process of choosing electors from the National Archives: **https://www.archives.gov/electoral-college/electors#selection**

New Jersey's electors voted for Barack Obama and Joe Biden in December 2008.

WINNER TAKES ALL

Most states give all of their electoral votes to the winner of the state's popular vote. The District of Columbia does this too. They follow the **winner takes all** rule.

If the Republican candidate wins, all the Republican electors go to the state capitol to vote. If the Democratic candidate wins, all the Democratic electors go.

Two states, Maine and Nebraska, have **proportional representation**. They split the votes. Two votes go to the winner of the state's popular vote. The rest go to the winner in each congressional district. Maine has two districts. Nebraska has three.

HIGH-STAKES CALIFORNIA

California follows the winner takes all rule. Even if a candidate wins by a very small amount, they still get all 55 of California's electoral votes. Candidates want to win California because its 55 votes can push them to victory.

PROPORTIONAL STATES

In 2008, Nebraska gave one district vote to Barack Obama and the other four to John McCain. In 2016, Maine gave one district vote to Donald Trump and one to Hillary Clinton.

People vote in Ohio, a winner-takes-all state.

OOPS! I CHANGED MY MIND

The Constitution doesn't say electors have to vote for any given candidate. Most states and the District of Columbia require electors to vote for the winner of the state's popular vote. Electors who don't may get in trouble.

A **faithless elector** doesn't vote for the person their state chose. These people may dislike the candidate. They may be protesting something about the election.

RECENT FAITHLESS ELECTORS

1976: Republican Mike Padden (opposed Gerald Ford)

1988: Democrat Margaret Leach, West Virginia (opposed Michael Dukakis)

2000: Democrat Barbara Lett-Simmons, District of Columbia (refused to vote)

2016: Republican Christopher Suprun, Texas (opposed Donald Trump)

✅ **VERIFIED**

FairVote, an organization that supports voting reform, has a page about faithless electors: **https://www.fairvote.org/faithless_electors**

Faithless elector Christopher Suprun speaks at a rally.

In 2016, Colorado elector Michael Baca should have voted for Hillary Clinton. He voted for John Kasich. The state threw out his vote. In 2019, a court ruled that Colorado couldn't do this. This was the first court ruling on electors' rights.

LOSING WHILE WINNING

A presidential candidate may win the popular vote but lose the election.

In 2000, Al Gore lost to George W. Bush. Gore received 500,000 more votes. In 2016, Hillary Clinton lost to Donald Trump. Clinton received several million more votes. Bush and Trump both received more electoral votes.

Two earlier presidents also won the electoral vote but not the popular vote: Rutherford B. Hayes (1876) and Benjamin Harrison (1888).

A protestor reminds electors that Hillary Clinton won the 2016 popular vote.

IS THE ELECTORAL COLLEGE FAIR?

Many people think the Electoral College is unfair. They say it's undemocratic. It suggests that citizens can't be trusted to pick their leaders. They say it's unfair that the winner of the popular vote can still lose the election.

The winner-takes-all style means candidates don't campaign in most states. They ignore small states with few electoral votes. They even ignore large states if they don't think they can win.

Candidates focus on the few states that might swing the election. **Swing states** have many electoral votes. These are states that could vote for either party.

The Electoral College might also seem unfair if the candidates tie. In this case, the House of Representatives chooses the president. Each state would get one vote.

Many people don't think it's fair that swing states get most of the attention from presidential candidates.

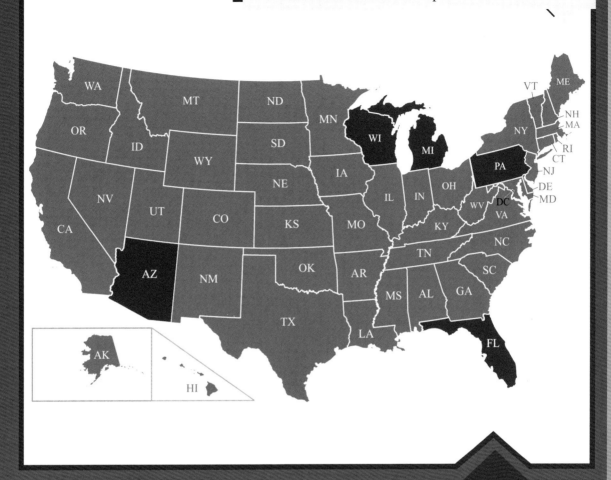

SWING STATES

For the 2020 election, the likely swing states are:
- Arizona
- Florida
- Michigan
- Pennsylvania
- Wisconsin

WEIRD THINGS CAN HAPPEN

When electoral votes are counted, members of Congress may object to individual votes. They can even object to an entire state's vote. They make the objection in writing. It must be signed by at least one senator and one representative.

The joint session then takes a break. The Senate and House consider the objection. Each group votes on whether to accept the objection. If both groups agree to the objection, the vote is thrown out. If either group disagrees, the vote is kept.

Sometimes, there is no clear winner. Votes may be tied. Or the winner may receive a **plurality**. This means they got the most votes but not a majority. In this case, the House of Representatives chooses the president.

OBJECTION NOT COUNTED

Objections to electoral votes were raised in 1969 and 2005. Both times, the objections were thrown out and the electoral votes were counted as normal.

TIED PRESIDENTIAL ELECTIONS

Only two presidential elections have been decided by the House:

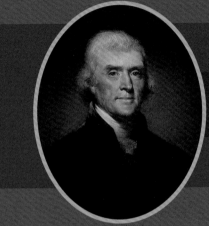

1800

THOMAS JEFFERSON

JOHN ADAMS

1824

JOHN Q. ADAMS

ANDREW JACKSON

There hasn't been a tied presidential election in around 200 years.

WHAT THE ELECTORAL COLLEGE DOESN'T DO

The Electoral College wasn't made to protect states' rights. The founders didn't want to give states the power to choose or remove the president. They wanted the president to be independent.

The founders didn't fear the popular vote. They rejected it for reasons that no longer apply.

First, southern states didn't want the North to have too much power. They fought to have slaves added to their population numbers. The end of slavery removed that reason for fearing the popular vote.

Second, the founders feared that voters didn't have enough information to vote. Today, voters are educated. They can learn about candidates online or in newspapers.

James Madison helped write the Constitution.
He later became the fourth president.

WHY WE STILL HAVE AN ELECTORAL COLLEGE

Americans want to be sure they elect the president fairly. In other words, they want a lawful election. The Constitution says this occurs when a candidate wins the Electoral College.

A candidate may win a plurality but not a majority. This can happen when there are third-party candidates. Even without a majority, the candidate who wins the Electoral College is the **legitimate** president.

Popular vote totals can be very close. The Electoral College results are often clearer.

Candidates have to work hard for electoral votes. They must consider all types of voters. This includes voters in cities and on farms. It includes **minority** voters, including African Americans, Asian Americans, and Hispanics.

Debates help voters choose their candidate. Here, George W. Bush and Al Gore debate.

WHICH RESULTS ARE BEST?

In 2000, Al Gore won 48.38 percent of the popular vote. George Bush won 47.87 percent. Bush got 271 electoral votes and won. Hillary Clinton won 48.2 percent of the 2016 popular vote. Donald Trump got just 46.1 percent. Trump received 306 electoral votes and won.

HOW PLURALITIES MESS UP ELECTIONS

In 1992, Democrat Bill Clinton won only 43.0 percent of the popular vote. Republican George H. W. Bush received 37.5 percent. Third-party candidate Ross Perot got 19 percent.

Clinton received 370 electoral votes. Bush got 168. Perot received none. The Electoral College made Clinton a legitimate president.

This may be the Electoral College's greatest strength. With more than two candidates, the highest popular vote-getter may have only a plurality. The Electoral College makes the winner legitimate.

The popularity of third-party candidate Ross Perot meant Bill Clinton won only by a plurality.

ROSS
PEROT

WILL THE ELECTORAL COLLEGE BE ABOLISHED OR CHANGED?

A **constitutional amendment** would be needed to **abolish** the Electoral College. This would require the votes of two-thirds of the House of Representatives and the Senate. Three-fourths of the states must also agree. This is highly unlikely to happen.

The Electoral College could be changed instead of removed. One different voting method is a state **compact**. In this system, states would give their electoral votes to the winner of the popular vote. Even if that candidate loses in their state, they'd get the votes. This can happen only if enough states agree.

Not everyone likes the state compact idea. They say it may not be fair.

PUSHING FOR A COMPACT

The state compact method is called the National Popular Vote Interstate Compact (NPVIC). A group of activists suggested it after the close 2000 election.

PASSED INTO LAW

PENDING PASSING

NO BILL PENDING

The map shows states that have passed or are considering NPVIC laws.

✔ VERIFIED

This is the official site for the National Popular Vote, an organization pushing to remove the Electoral College:
https://www.nationalpopularvote.com

WHAT WOULD REPLACE THE ELECTORAL COLLEGE?

There are several ways to replace the Electoral College. Each has strengths and weaknesses.

In a direct popular vote, each person gets one vote. The candidate with the most votes wins. This candidate may win by a plurality. Some people don't like that.

In two-round voting, the winner always has a majority. During the first round, people vote for one among all candidates. During the second round, they pick from the top two.

In ranked-choice voting, voters rank all the candidates. A candidate receiving a majority of first-rank votes wins. Otherwise, the candidate with the fewest first-choice votes is removed. Those votes go to each voter's second-choice candidate. Finally, one candidate receives a majority.

France successfully used a two-round voting system in 2017.

Ensemble, la France !
7 MAI 2017

TWO ROUNDS IN FRANCE

France's 2017 presidential election used two-round voting. In round one, Emmanuel Macron received 24 percent of the vote. Marine Le Pen received 21 percent. Other candidates received fewer votes. In round two, Le Pen got 33 percent. Macron received 66 percent and won.

VOTING FOR THE FUTURE

The Electoral College elects only the U.S. president and vice president. These are the country's highest elected offices.

The winners of this election can change the nation. The president decides how the country acts on a lot of issues. These include health care, education, and immigration.

The president sets the tone for how the country and its people behave. Elections for this office must be fair. They must be legitimate. The person who wins should be chosen by the people. However, not every vote is equal. This is why people are discussing the Electoral College. Should it be removed? Should it be changed? Should it be replaced? What do you think?

VERIFIED

You can find out more about voting in the United States here:
https://www.usa.gov/voting-laws

The president's job is very important. They lead the country for its people.

GLOSSARY

abolish To officially end or stop something.

candidate A person running for an elected office.

compact An agreement or contract, usually between two or more states.

compromise An agreement in which each person or group gives up something in order to end a dispute.

constitutional amendment An addition to the U.S. Constitution that changes its meaning.

elector A member of the Electoral College, which is the group that elects the president and vice president of the United States.

electoral vote The votes cast by all the members of the Electoral College.

faithless elector An elector who promises to vote for a certain candidate and then does not.

joint session A meeting of the Senate and House of Representatives together.

legitimate Lawfully and legally elected.

majority More than half of the votes cast in an election.

minority Making up less than half of a group or a vote.

plurality A vote count in which a candidate receives the most votes, but less than a majority.

popular vote The votes of the general population of a place.

proportional representation The method where a state splits its electoral votes based on winners of congressional districts.

swing state A state whose vote is divided and could change the outcome of an election.

winner takes all The method where the winner of the popular vote gets all of a state's electoral votes.

INDEX